A Dose of Awkward

Left-Handed Toons
(by Right-Handed People)

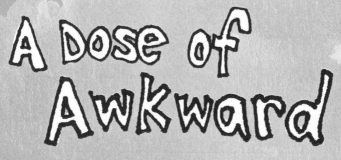

Drew Mokris
& Justin Boyd

HOW
BOOKS
Cincinnati, Ohio
www.howdesign.com

For more excellent books and resources for designers, visit www.howdesign.com.

13 12 11 10 09   5 4 3 2 1

Distributed in Canada by Fraser Direct, 100 Armstrong Avenue, Georgetown, Ontario, Canada L7G 5S4, Tel: (905) 877-4411. Distributed in the U.K. and Europe by David & Charles, Brunel House, Newton Abbot, Devon, TQ12 4PU, England, Tel: (+44) 1626-323200, Fax: (+44) 1626-323319, E-mail: postmaster@davidandcharles.co.uk. Distributed in Australia by Capricorn Link, P.O. Box 704, Windsor, NSW 2756 Australia, Tel: (02) 4577-3555.

Library of Congress Cataloging-in-Publication Data

Mokris, Drew.
  [Left-handed toons (by right-handed people). Selections]
  A dose of awkward : Left-handed toons (by right-handed people) / Drew Mokris & Justin Boyd.
    p. cm.
  Summary: "This book covers our favorite comics from the first two years of our website"--Introd.
  ISBN 978-1-60061-303-6 (pbk. : alk. paper)
  1. American wit and humor, Pictorial. 2. Left- and right-handedness. I. Boyd, Justin. II. Title.
III. Title: Left-handed toons (by right-handed people).
  NC1429.M69A4 2009
  741.5'973--dc22
                              2009019955

Edited by Amy Schell
Designed by Claudean Wheeler
Page layout by Grace Ring
Production coordinated by Greg Nock

Acknowledgments

Thank you to Mom, Dad, Natalie and all the dogs.

—DREW

Thank you Mom, Dad and Cara for your support. Thanks Drew for that one time you picked me up from the airport. Wait, did you ever pick me up from the airport? Never mind.

—JUSTIN

Originally from Michigan, Justin Boyd moved to New York with his family when he was 12, only to return to get his BSE in Computer Science from the University of Michigan. After he graduated in 2006, he went back east to work in New York City as a software engineer.

When he's at home, he plays a very down-tuned electric guitar, writing music whenever inspiration strikes. Video games are another favorite pastime for the rare moment when Justin isn't working on a cartoon, a song or a programming side-project.

Justin has a very interesting relationship with food. One time, he ate a gallon of ice cream in one sitting. For fun. Another time in college, he accidentally went three entire days without eating because of sleeping in, classes and extreme procrastination on assignments. During Superbowl XLI, he ate over 5,000 calories of food just because someone challenged him to do it. That someone was himself.

Justin was really short when he was a child. Now, he is just kinda short. He is ¼ Japanese. In high school, he worked at the Gap and still religiously folds shirts and pants Gap style. Even if they're not his.

Justin

ABOUT Drew

Drew grew up in Michigan, where his mom taught him how to draw. Years later, Drew started recording voicemail messages his mother left him, then he animated them with cartoon penguins, and she became the unwitting star of the series, "Penguin Calls." These appeared alongside other animations about dumb dinosaurs and tiny plaid ninjas on Drew's first website, www.spinnerdisc.com.

Drew went to University of Michigan and studied computer engineering, and now he is a programmer during the week. During the weekend, he is still a programmer, just one that isn't at work. The time available to make flash cartoons has waned, but the time available to doodle nonsense on paper remains.

Drew is tall. Kinda. He wears glasses. He doesn't like odd numbers because they are inherently angry and days of the week have colors in his brain. Drew is proud that his name is a verb, but he does not respond to "past tense of draw." He is also proud his crippling case of Internet-addiction has given him a forum to present his art.

Drew

TABLE OF CONTENTS

Welcome

It started out as just a simple gimmick, but it has morphed into something much more than that. Who knew that drawing silly cartoons with a non-dominant left hand would yield such results! What used to only exist on the web has now made it into book form, and all because of a simple concept. It didn't just happen overnight though; it has been several years in the making.

Both Drew and I went to the University of Michigan and after we graduated in 2006, entered the lady-filled world of software engineering. My first job had a lot of downtime, so I started making silly comics to pass the time. I've never been an amazing artist, so I asked Drew to redraw the comics and possibly post them somewhere. Drew wasn't really up for that because he liked the style of the comics, so I suggested that he redraw them with his left hand, so that they were still messy. That's when we both realized, "Hey, both of us should draw our ideas lefty and make a webcomic out of it!"

And voila! On January 14th, 2007, LefthandedToons.com was born, where we alternately post comics drawn awkwardly with our left hands. This book covers our favorite comics from the first two years of our website.

LefthandedToons.com has always been where all of the weird thoughts in my head end up. Instead of saying them out loud and possibly getting very strange looks, I just make a comic out of it. Simple. And it makes me appear more normal to the people that are around me every day. Except my girlfriend: She ends up hearing every strange thought that goes through my head. But she knows I'm not normal.

—JUSTIN BOYD

Introduction

Yes, Welcome

I think of this as an experiment with no meaningful conclusion. Also, we don't really have a hypothesis to prove. And I guess we just made up the procedure as we went along, and there isn't any data to analyze. This is like an experiment without any scientific rigor.

Since I've known Justin, he's always made me laugh. We almost got kicked out of class once for it. (The drawing we were passing back and forth eventually became a comic in this book.) LefthandedToons.com has been a way for us both to tap into that messy-funny-doodle lobe of the brain. It's the lobe right next to the one that stores TV theme songs from 1994. Take a right at the id. You can't miss it.

Though the non-dominant hand adapts after a while, it's never quite the same as drawing with your dominant hand. The left hand produces a certain slanted surrealism when it's given a pen. Wrong-handed drawing is like being a member of synchronized swimming team, except you're blindfolded. And your right hand is actually your left hand, and also the rest of the team are penguins. It's exactly like that.

We're just nerds with a gimmick. Sometimes we collaborate, discussing ideas and characters, but usually the toons are thrown at the world with as little personal deliberation as possible. These comics are supposed to be free and messy. Like a toddler. These comics are exactly like a toddler. A toddler who's right-handed but who's drawing comics with his left hand. And who's great with metaphors.

—DREW MOKRIS

2

CHAPTER 1

Quirks

it's such a nice day. i hope a meteor doesn't hit earth or anything
knock on wood! knock on wood!
there is no wood around! we're in a field!
why do we always have to hang out in fields?!
do something!
gee, thanks a lot

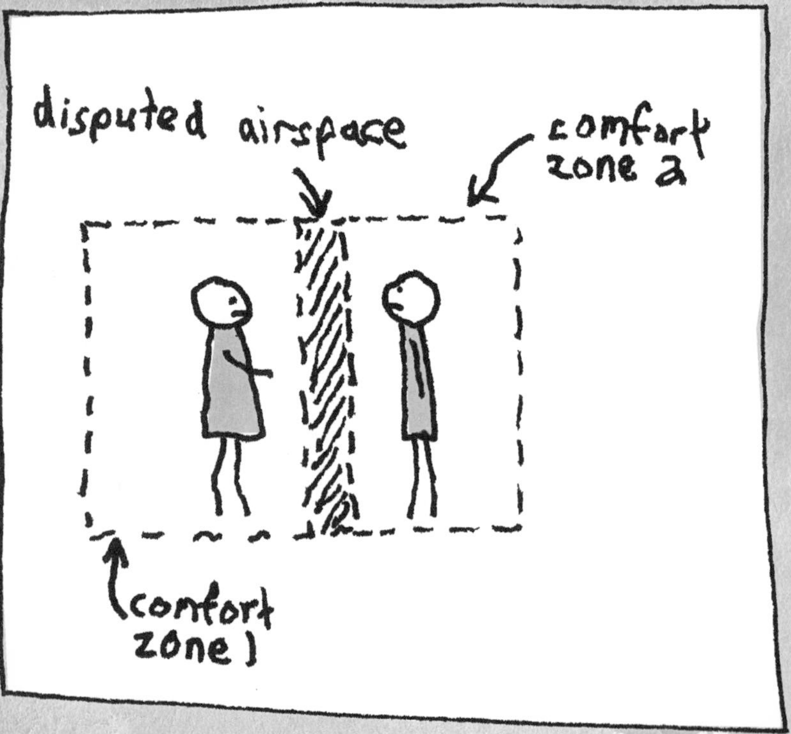
disputed airspace
comfort zone 2
comfort zone 1

"I CARRED TO THE TRAIN,
THEN I TRAINED TO THE SEA!
TURNING NOUNS INTO VERBS
IS MY PROVERBIAL TEA!"

"WELL I'M SICK WITH SOME TIREDS.
IF I HAVE ANGRIES, FORGIVE."
(verbing nouns can be nice...
I'd rather noun adjectives.)

Quirks

ha! my beard is better than your beard!
im 7!
So
and a girl
listen, this is the only way i can win this game. just bear with me.

PATRICK HAS A DARK SECRET.

I HIGHLIGHT ALL THE TEXT ON EVERY WEBSITE I VISIT.

I ALWAYS THOUGHT "KNICKS" CAME FROM A LITERAL PRONUNCIATION OF "NYC", BUT APPARENTLY IT COMES FROM "KNICKERBOCKERS"!

BUT REALLY, FOR ALL SUPER-BULLDOGS, I THINK WE CAN ASSUME—

"INTENTS AND PURPOSES".

HUH?

I THINK YOU MEANT TO SAY, "INTENTS AND PURPOSES".

WHAT DID I SAY?

"SUPER-BULLDOGS"

OH, WHOOPS! I ALWAYS DO THAT!

I KNOW

Quirks

Great Interview Tips

Tip #14: Make good
eye contact.

YOUR EYEBALL IS
PHYSICALLY TOUCHING
MY EYEBALL...

...YOU'RE HIRED.

Great Interview Tips

Tip #15: Tout your strengths on your résumé.

Shampoo Call Center Script

Problem: Caller has run out of shampoo

Q1: Are you sure?

Q2: Have you been leaving it upside down after use?

Q3: Have you filled it with some water and shaken it?

If still unresolved, suggest buying more

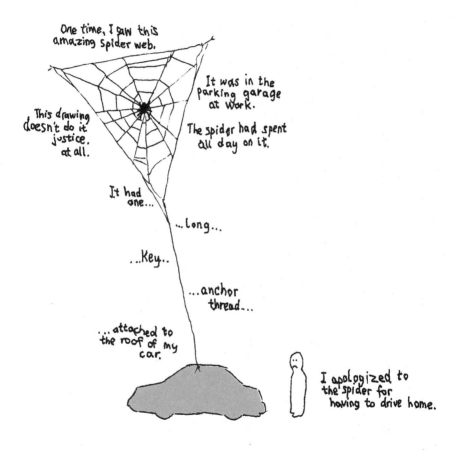

One time, I saw this amazing spider web.

It was in the parking garage at work.

The spider had spent all day on it.

This drawing doesn't do it justice. at all.

It had one...

...long...

...Key..

...anchor thread...

...attached to the roof of my car.

I apologized to the spider for having to drive home.

2

Irks

In the upcoming election season, be sure to find out where candidates stand on issues that are important to you.

DECORATIONS ARE UP.

I WANT A DIVORCE.

I FIND MYSELF PERTURBED BY THE OCCURRENCE OF TELEVISION ADVERTISEMENTS BEFORE THE FEATURE FILM AT MY LOCAL CINEMA.

VERILY, I PRESUME MY EMPATHY ON THE MATTER WILL DO LITTLE TO EASE YOUR PERTURBATION, YOU PERFECT ASS.

IRKED WORMS

A Poem to my Alarm Clock

I promise to never ask "where?"
I only will ask you "when?"
And you seem to be partially aware
That I prefer my numbers base-<u>ten</u>.

But when a<u>larmed</u>, I've noticed, perhaps,
You refuse to allow me to choose...
It's always <u>nine</u> minutes elapsed,
'Til again you allow me to snooze.

THE FACT IS, THE ECONOMY IS IN A SORRY STATE, AND MY OPPONENT HAS NOT DONE ENOUGH TO AMELIORATE IT!

I THINK MY CONSTITUENTS WILL AGREE THAT OUR POLICIES ARE MORE THAN ADEQUATE IN MOST SITUATIONS.

SEE? "MOST SITUATIONS." THE RELIANCE UPON SUCH QUALIFIERS IS AN ADMISSION THAT THE SENATOR'S SOLUTION IS INCOMPLETE!

EXCUSE ME?! CAULIFLOWERS?! NOW, I'VE ENDURED A LOT OF MUD-SLINGING, BUT NO ONE'S EVER ACCUSED ME OF RELYING UPON CAULIFLOWERS!!

I DIDN'T SAY "CAULIFLOWERS", IDIOT. I SAID "QUALIFIERS"!

OH!! WELL I THOUGHT YOU SAID "CAULIFLOWERS", OKAY?!!?!

CAN I PLEASE HEAR THE WORD IN A SENTENCE PLEASE?

YEAH FINE. "INSUFFERABLE":... I FIND THE OTHER KID LEFT TO BE LESS INSUFFERABLE.

Question: Why, while waiting for a green light so you can turn left, would you inch forward?

Answer: To block my view when I'm trying to turn right on red.

WHAT IS YOUR FREAKING PROBLEM?!

is this the right room?
nope. the big head, little body meeting is down the hall

Irks

i like your tie
oh
i'm actually not wearing one
it just so happened that my coffee spill this morning made a stain in the exact shape of a tie

3

Friends/ Jerks

SO, SEE, IT TURNS OUT "FRUITYLOOPS" IS A COMPUTER PROGRAM, BUT I THOUGHT HE WAS TALKING ABOUT SOMETHING ELSE ENTIRELY!

WHOA. WAIT. HAVE YOU BEEN TALKING TO ME THIS WHOLE TIME?

REALLY? WOW! JESUS!

SERIOUSLY, SHUT THE HELL UP.

SUPER BEST FRIENDS!!

CLAP!

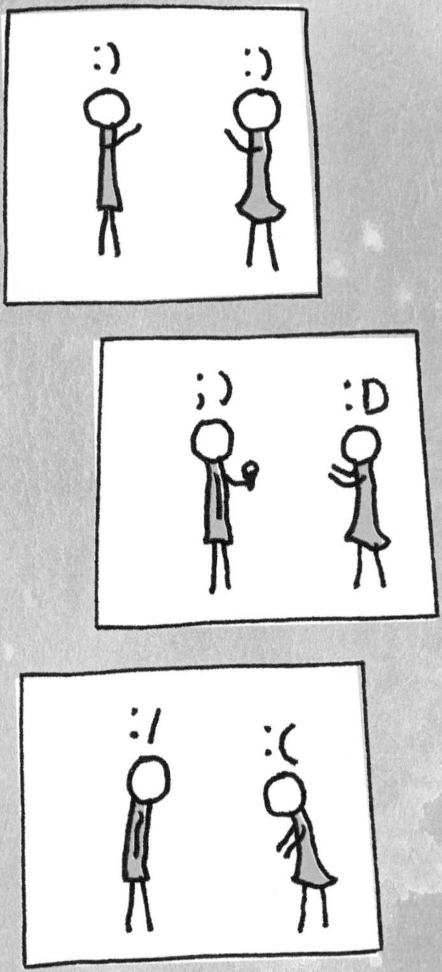
:)
:)
;)
:D
:/
:(

HEY HEY!
GUESS WHAT
I'M DOING!

I'M JAYWALKING!
HA HA!!

LAAAME.

BUT...
BUT I HAD
DISFIGURING
SURGERY!!

I MAKE SOME PEOPLE SNEEZE!

sweet dance move! what's it called?
im actually having a controlled seizure
stop dancing and please help me!

Chapter 3

Sometimes, pillows can
help you go to sleep

forever

WILL SMITH

JIGGY.

Holds a press
conference

AS THE NEW WILLENIUM GOES ON, I AM WORRIED ABOUT WILLITARY SPENDING, WHILE WILLIONS OF AMERICANS CAN'T AFFORD FOOD OR MY ALBUMS. QUESTIONS?

I THOUGHT YOU LOOKED FUNNY IN "I, ROBOT" WITH A GOATEE BUT NO MOUSTACHE.

THAT'S NOT WILLY A QUESTION.

I KNOW.

Friends/Jerks

something is wrong with your food. it killed frank.
he's just being dramatic
eat
i must not be very good at cooking

i just found out something!
what's that?
watch
i can emit a powerful laser out of my
oh, whoops

CHAPTER 4

Time-Out Chair

How to Play
Cat's Cradle

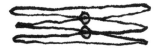

grab at the circled
points, pull to the
outside, then quickly
throw string in the
trash

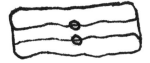

at the circled
points, cut the string
and never play this
game again

Of Love And Apples

The girls, they would play it at every lunch break.
They'd giggle and laugh and make noises kids make.

Pull the stem off the apple, just by twisting it.
With each twist say a letter from the alphabet.

And the letter that popped it, that was the key!
Twas the first initial of the boy she fancied.

"A...B...C...D...E..." - and off comes the stem.
"Ewww! You like Evan! Oooh, I'm gonna tell him!"

The red fruit had spoken! And so went the game.
And they'd play it the next day: new stems meant new names.

And poor Zachary...

There wasn't an apple in the whole stupid world !
With a strong enough stem to secure him a girl.

BEER SOLVES PROBLEMS.

i think being a third wheel is actually a compliment. once you have three wheels, you could possibly be a Big Wheel, and that is awesome.

Time-Out Chair

sure, i can help you with your science project, but what can you do for me?
don't you love me?
love doesn't pay the bills son

CHAPTER 5

Weird Science

check out the revolutionary new weight loss plan thats sweeping the nation!

i lost 15 pounds in a matter of seconds!

i lost over 50 pounds over the course of a weekend!

my plan is changing lives everywhere and i guarantee the weight will never come back.

i came up with the plan myself

it's called "a limb a day"

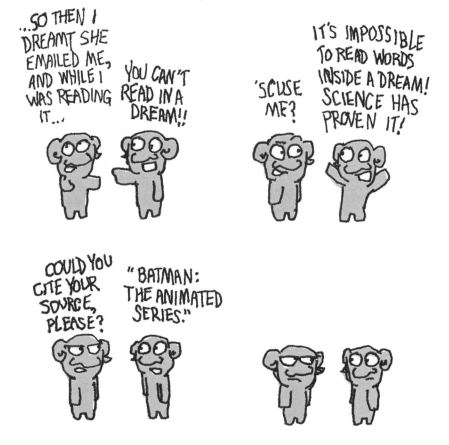

BEFORE YOU MAY KISS THE BRIDE, YOU MUST CHANGE YOUR FACEBOOK STATUS TO "MARRIED" SO THIS THING IS OFFICIAL.

Weird Science

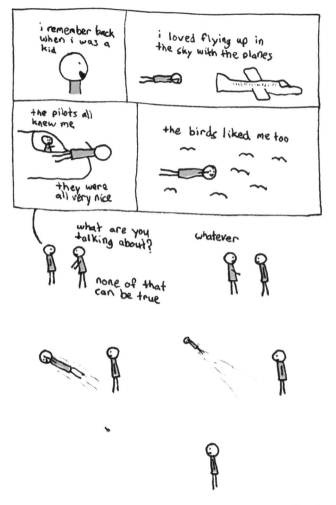

Poor Basebot.

Weird Science

Y'SEE, THE MOON'S ORBITAL PERIOD EQUALS ITS ROTATIONAL PERIOD. THAT'S WHY THE SAME SIDE IS ALWAYS FACING US.

THE OTHER SIDE OF THE MOON, WHICH WE NEVER GET TO SEE FROM EARTH, LOOKS DIFFERENT. IT KINDA JUST HAS ONE BIG OL' CRATER.

WE ALWAYS SEE THE "MAN IN THE MOON".

THEY SAY IF THE FAR SIDE OF THE MOON WERE THE ONE FACING US, WE MIGHT HAVE A WHOLE DIFFERENT MYTHOLOGY ABOUT IT. MAYBE IT WOULD LOOK LIKE A GIANT EYE IN THE SKY.

OR A BUTTHOLE.

YEAH, OR A BUTTHOLE.

Hey it's time for a
THOUGHT-PRO-VOKAL!

HEY I'M
AN OWL!

What monsters scared
YOU as a kid?

a. boogeyman

b. aliens-that-got-ray guns

c. unscrupulous investment bankers

d. cookie

Feel free to shout your
answer or something i don't know.

6

Romantic/ Hopeless

oh my god! 5 minutes into the date and i've already run out of things to say!
stay calm.., stay calm. i got it!
somebody find a doctor!!! help!!!
nice. this will be a funny story we can tell our kids someday

WHOA! WHAT HAPPENED TO YOU?

I MET THIS AMAZING, BEAUTIFUL GIRL ON THE TRAIN, AND I FELL IN LOVE.

SO YOUR EYES TOOK ON A LITERAL HEART SHAPE?

IT'S VERY PAINFUL!

LOVE HURTS!

YES IT DOES.

YES IT DOES.

Chapter 6

This man is **HEAD OVER HEELS** → IT TURNS OUT IT'S NOT THAT BIG A DEAL.

i dont think i can use that dating site anymore
why is that?
my dad uses it too
who cares!
we both ended up dating the same person
oh. thats gross

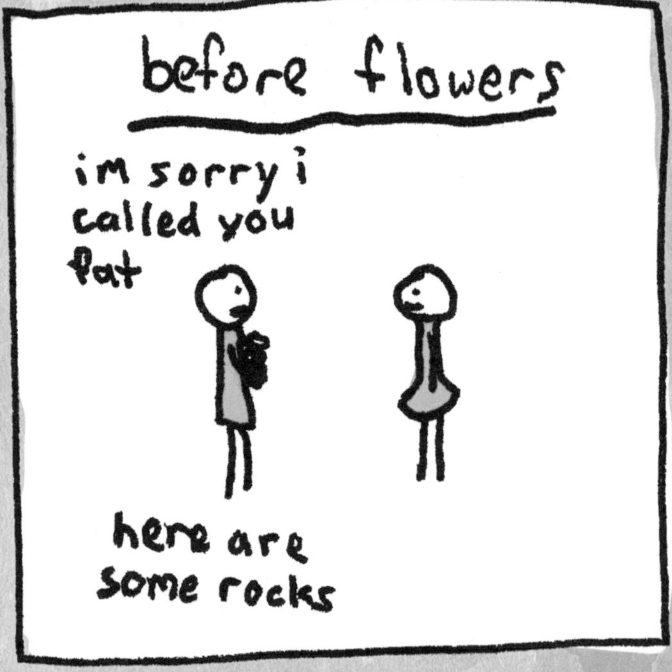
before flowers
im sorry i called you fat
here are some rocks

before glaring

i wish there was a
way to show how angry
i am with you just by
looking at you

Dear pretty-girls-who-
wear-big-sunglasses,

I think you look silly.

you should have an excuse for being that ugly sir
i'm a woman!
that doesn't make it any better

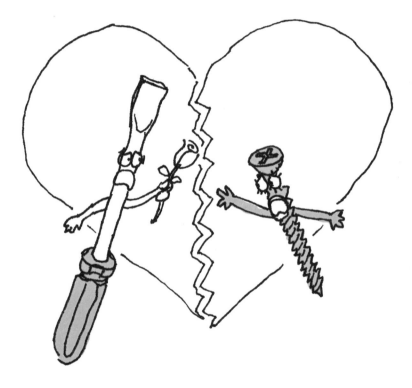

7

Fighting Words

"NINTENDO WII" IS ACTUALLY THE PLURAL FORM OF "NINTENDO WIUS."

Fighting Words

Octagon and Nonagon
    Sat on a bale of hay,
When Octy yawned, "We oughta gone
    To the mall today."
But Nonagon remained withdrawn;
    No comments on the mall.
Cuz all along, the nonagon
    was not a gon at all.

Fighting Words

Y'KNOW, "BISEXUAL" IS A POORLY-FORMED WORD. I THINK IT SHOULD BE "AMBISEXUAL", BECAUSE "AMBI-" MEANS "BOTH", AND THERE ARE ONLY TWO SEXES.

"BI-" MEANS TWO, WHICH IMPLIES WE COULD USE OTHER NUMERIC PREFIXES. BUT WHAT, FOR EXAMPLE, WOULD A "QUADRISEXUAL" BE??

HEY! MY UNCLE IS A QUADRISEXUAL!

YOUR UNCLE IS NOT A QUADRISEXUAL. HE IS AN AIRLINE PILOT.

YEAH. THAT'S WHAT I MEANT.

HE FLIES IN BIG PLANES!!

Chapter 7

TODAY'S WORD: "ITALY"

THE NAME OF THE NATION OF **ITALY** COMES FROM THE LATIN WORD, "ITALLUS," WHICH MEANS "TO LEAN, SLANT, OR FALL OVER." THERE ARE SEVERAL THEORIES AS TO HOW THIS BECAME TODAY'S "ITALY."

ONE THEORY ASSERTS THE NAME STUCK AS A DESCRIPTOR OF THE COUNTRY'S ARCHITECTURE.

ANOTHER THEORY SUGGESTS THAT ANCIENT CARTOGRAPHERS NOTICED ITALY'S RESEMBLANCE TO THE LEG OF A MAN TRIPPING ON THE ISLAND OF SICILY.

WHATEVER THE ORIGIN, THERE IS MODERN USAGE OF "ITALLUS" THAT HAS SURVIVED, AND THAT IS IN THE NAME OF THE SLANTED FONT-STYLE USED FOR EMPHASIS:

italics

WOW, CRAP, GUYS. DOES THAT SOUND REAL? I TOTALLY JUST MADE THAT ALL UP.

Fighting Words

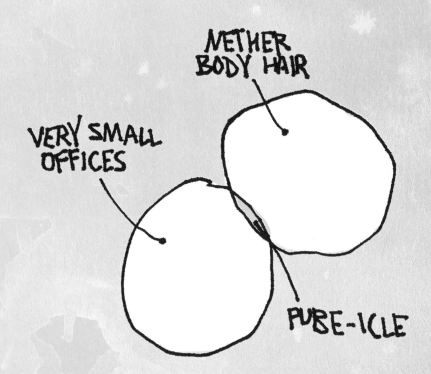

NETHER
BODY HAIR

VERY SMALL
OFFICES

PUBE-ICLE

FORE!!!

nice shot!

you hit that guy right in the face!

what's the golf equivalent of a triple word score, because that's what that just was

Today's Word: "Basketball"

IT'S WIDELY BELIEVED THAT "BASKETBALL" GETS ITS NAME FROM THE BASKET-SHAPED GOAL.

IN FACT, THE REVERSE IS TRUE.

LET'S START WITH THE LATIN, "BASKUS", WHICH MEANS "TO SLEEP" OR "TO LIE".

"BASK LIZARDS" GET THEIR NAME FROM THIS WORD, DUE TO THEIR LETHARGIC BEHAVIOR.

IN MELBOURNE, AUSTRALIA, WHERE BASKETBALL WAS INVENTED IN 1824, BASK LIZARD SKINS PROVIDED THE PERFECT COVERING FOR THE GAME BALL.

"BASKBALL" BECAME POPULAR VERY QUICKLY.

ONLY LATER DID THE "BASKET" GOAL LEND ITS NAME TO OTHER SIMILAR OBJECTS.

THAT THING THAT HOLDS FRUIT ON YOUR TABLE? IT'S NAMED AFTER SLEEPY LIZARDS.

8

Um, What?

EXTREME!

Um, What?

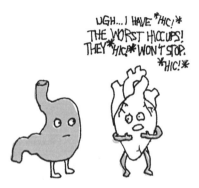

Um, What?

Um, What?

Um, What?

Chapter 8

before gravity

Um, What?

Um, What?

AND SO, THE TRAGEDY COULDN'T BE AVOIDED. NOW, WE THROW IT OVER TO JAKE WITH SPORTS.

THANKS, ALAN! TODAY IN SPORTS, SOMETIMES THEY TRIED TO KEEP THE BALL FROM TOUCHING THE GROUND, AND IN OTHER SPORTSGAMES, YOU'RE SUPPOSED TO MAKE THE BALL TOUCH THE GROUND SOMETIMES.

BACK TO YOU, ALAN!

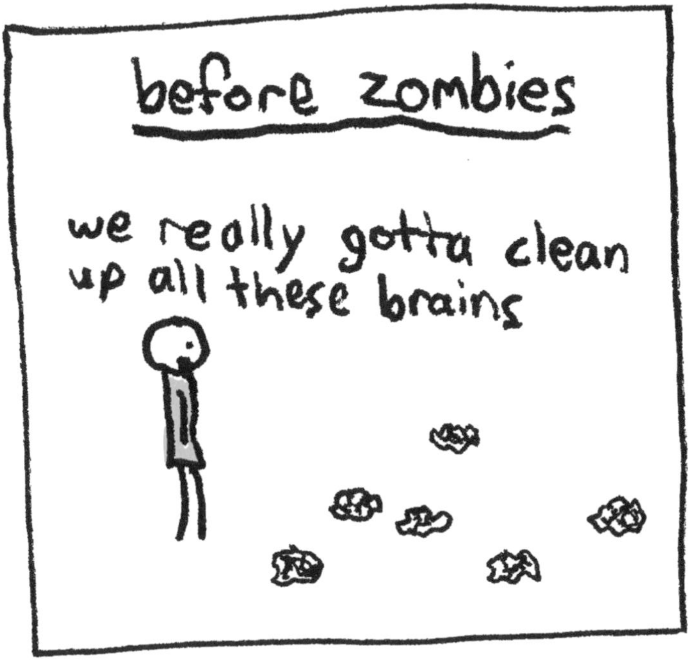
before zombies
we really gotta clean up all these brains

BABY
RABIES!

BRABIES!

Chapter 8

Potatoes: The meat of vegetables.

YOU. YOU'RE IN.

false

in 2007, neckties were responsible for 90% of workplace deaths

this man's tie got caught on his desk when he fell out of his chair

this man's tie got stuck in the shredder

do you want to support a product that kills people?

paid for by the national bowtie association

Don't let this happen.

Don't wear bowties.

brought to you by Neckties For Love™

Um, What?

OKAY, WE'RE ALL SET MR. ...AGLICK.

THAT'S PRONOUNCED "MAGICK".

OH...I'M SORRY. WE HAVE IT SPELLED "A-G-L-I-C-K" HERE.

THAT'S RIGHT. THE "L" IS SILENT.

AND THE "M" IS INVISIBLE.

WOOOOOOOOOOOO

my arms fell off last week
i still haven't figured out a way to put them back on

MORE GREAT TITLES FROM
HOW Books

ZOMBIE HAIKU

Zombie Haiku will keep you up late into the night. It's the touching (albeit cold and clammy) story of a zombie's gradual decay, told through the intimate poetry of haiku. From infection to demise, you'll trod along the journey through deserted streets and barricaded doors for every eye-popping, gut-wrenching, flesh-eating moment.

#Z1805, 144 pages, paperback, ISBN: 978-1-60061-070-7

MILK EGGS VODKA

If we are what we eat, then *Milk Eggs Vodka* reveals deep truths about the average American with over 150 found grocery lists, including everything from the mundane to the marginally insane. The book also includes short essays on collecting, shopping, eating, and list-making, and even some recipes that can be made from the ingredients on certain lists. Tasty.

#Z0675, 240 pages, hardcover, ISBN: 978-1-58180-941-1

KAWAII NOT

What exactly is *kawaii*? Well, kawaii is the Japanese term for "cute" (as in, "look at the fuzzy kitten, he's so kawaii") and not is an English term meaning "not." Explore the darker side of cute with this fun collection of quirky comic strips. Each strip is perforated, so you can rip it out and give it to a friend or stick it on your fridge. Also includes stickers!

#Z1845, 208 pages, paperback, ISBN: 978-1-60061-076-9

 Find these and other fine HOW Books titles at your local bookstore or www.howbookstore.com.